The Three Musketeers

ALEXANDRE DUMAS

Level 2

Retold by Diane Mowat
Series Editors: Andy Hopkins and Jocelyn Potter

Pearson Education Limited
Edinburgh Gate, Harlow,
Essex CM20 2JE, England
and Associated Companies throughout the world.

ISBN 0 582 42113 6

This edition first published 2000

NEW EDITION

5 7 9 10 8 6 4

Typeset by Pantek Arts Ltd, Maidstone, Kent
Set in 11/14pt Bembo
Printed in China
SWTC/04

Published by Pearson Education Limited in association with
Penguin Books Ltd, both companies being subsidiaries of Pearson Plc

Acknowledgements:
Film Trust/Este Films (courtesy of The Kobal Coolection)
pp3, 15 and 31; Film Trust Productions (ciyrtest of
The Kobal Collectuib: pp 11 and 21

Every effort has been made to trace copyright holders
in every case. The publishers would be interested
to hear from any not acknowledged here.

For a complete list of titles available in the Penguin Readers series, please write to your local
Pearson Education office or to: Penguin Readers Marketing Department,
Pearson Education, Edinburgh Gate, Harlow, Essex CM20 2JE.

Contents

Introduction

'You can use a sword. You will fight well because you are a Gascon and my son. Fight when you are angry with somebody. But do not fight the King or the Cardinal!'

These are the words of young d'Artagnan's father, when his son leaves home for Paris. D'Artagnan wants to fight for his King and his country, but other fights come first. Who are the three musketeers, and why do they want to kill him? Why is the King angry with the Queen? Is the Cardinal the King's friend, or has he got other plans? And who is the beautiful 'Milady'?

Alexandre Dumas wrote *The Three Musketeers* in 1844, but everything in the story happened more than 200 years before that. Louis XIII was the King of France then, but he was very young. Cardinal Richelieu did nearly everything for him. When King Louis was fourteen, he married the daughter of the King of Spain. But for a time she was very friendly with the Duke of Buckingham, a friend of King Charles I of England.

The Duke of Buckingham tried to help the French Protestants. France was a Catholic country, but the Protestants took the city of La Rochelle from the King. The King and the Cardinal had to take the city back. The King's army used long guns – muskets. People with these guns were 'musketeers'.

Alexandre Dumas wrote a lot of books, and his most exciting stories are the most famous. *The Three Musketeers* and *The Count of Monte Cristo* are also films.

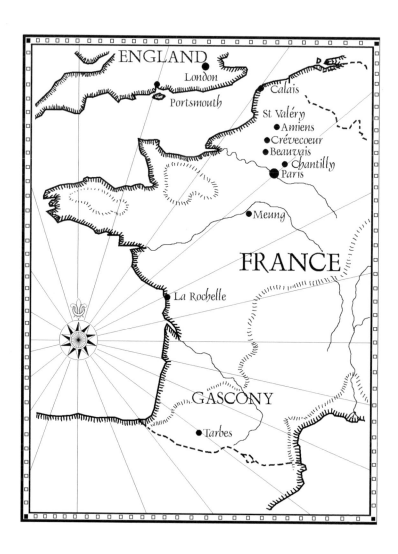

Chapter 1   At an Inn in Meung

'Well, all right,' said d'Artagnan's father. 'Go to Paris. You are only eighteen years old, but you are not a child. I cannot give you much money, but you can have my horse. And I will write a letter to my old friend, de Tréville. He is a Gascon★ too, and he and I were friends in the army. Now he is the captain of the King's musketeers.

'You can use a sword. You will fight well because you are a Gascon and my son. Fight when you are angry with somebody. But do not fight the King or the Cardinal!'

With these words, the older man gave his sword to his son. Then he turned away. He didn't want his son to see him cry.

D'Artagnan's mother cried too, but she didn't turn away. She gave her son a piece of paper.

'Keep this,' she told him. 'Look at it when you are ill. Take the things on it and you will feel better. Now please be careful!'

◆

Nothing happened between his home at Tarbes and the town of Meung, on the road to Paris, so d'Artagnan didn't have to use his sword.

At Meung, d'Artagnan stopped at the door of the biggest inn. He waited outside with his horse, and he looked round him. One of the windows of the inn was open, and inside d'Artagnan saw three men. They looked at d'Artagnan's horse and laughed.

'They are laughing at me,' d'Artagnan thought angrily. He called to them. 'What are you laughing at? When I see people laugh, I like to understand. Then I can laugh too.'

★ Gascon: a person from Gascony (Gascogne) in south-west France.

The most important man looked at d'Artagnan. 'I'm not talking to you,' he said.

When he heard this, d'Artagnan was more angry. He pulled his sword out, and he started to run into the inn.

But the innkeeper saw him. With three of his men, he attacked d'Artagnan. They had no swords, but the attack came from behind d'Artagnan. They hit him again and again on his head. He was on the ground before he could turn round.

They carried him into the kitchen. Then the innkeeper spoke to the important man.

'He is quiet now,' he said. 'He does not know anything. I do not think he is an important man. He hasn't much money and he only has one shirt. He has a letter with *To Monsieur de Tréville, Captain of the King's Musketeers* on it.

The innkeeper was right. D'Artagnan was very quiet. But he was a Gascon, and Gascons have hard heads. Five minutes later, he felt better and he was on his feet again. He went to the window and looked for the important man.

There, outside the inn, he saw him. He was by a big carriage with a young woman inside it. D'Artagnan could only see the young woman's head through the window of the carriage, but she was very beautiful. She was between twenty and twenty-two years old and she had large blue eyes, long hair and a beautiful face. She was talking quietly to the important man.

'So what does the Cardinal say?' she asked him.

'Go back to England now. When the Duke leaves London, tell the Cardinal.'

'Is that all?' asked the beautiful young woman.

'Open this box when you get to England.'

'All right. And what do you have to do?'

'I am going back to Paris.'

'No, you are not!' shouted d'Artagnan, and he ran out of the inn.

2

She had large blue eyes, long hair and a beautiful face.

The man's hand went to his sword, but the young woman in the carriage said, 'Remember the Cardinal's words!'

'The Cardinal,' thought d'Artagnan.

'You are right, Milady★,' said the man. 'We cannot wait.' He jumped on his horse, and the carriage driver started his horses. The carriage went one way, and the important man went the other way.

D'Artagnan started to run after him, but his head hurt. He fell down in the street.

'He will be here for a long time now,' said the innkeeper.

◆

He was wrong. D'Artagnan was up at five o'clock the next morning. He went down to the kitchen with his mother's piece of paper, and he found the right things. So, with his mother's help, d'Artagnan was nearly well again in the evening.

'Now,' he said to the innkeeper, 'where's my letter?'

'The other man took it from you yesterday,' the innkeeper answered. But he didn't really know the answer to d'Artagnan's question.

Chapter 2   The King's Musketeers

D'Artagnan found a room in Paris, and then he went to look for Monsieur de Tréville.

The captain of King Louis XIII's musketeers was easy to find. Everybody in the city knew him and his musketeers. The musketeers were nearly all men of good family. You could see them everywhere. They pushed past people. They shouted and

★ Milady: the French name for an important English woman.

4

made a lot of noise. They were loud and angry, but they were ready to give their lives for the King.

The most important man in France at the time was not the King; it was Cardinal Richelieu. The Cardinal also had guards. Each man wanted the strongest and the best guards. Monsieur de Tréville's men often pushed the Cardinal's guards in the street and then a fight began. The King and the Cardinal knew about the fights. The King was always happy when some of his musketeers were in a fight and won. The Cardinal was happy when his guards won.

◆

When d'Artagnan arrived at Monsieur de Tréville's house, he found a large number of musketeers there. They played a game on the stairs with their swords, and he watched. When one man hurt another musketeer, they all laughed loudly.

D'Artagnan asked for Monsieur de Tréville. Then he stood and waited. He looked round at the other men there. One very tall musketeer had a fine sword, and he talked about it loudly all the time.

'No, Porthos,' another musketeer said. 'You did not buy that sword with the money from your father. The woman at the Porte St Honoré gave it to you last Sunday.'

'I tell you, I did pay for it. Is that not right, Aramis?'

Aramis was quite different from his friend. He was young – perhaps twenty-three – with dark eyes and a kind face.

He spoke very little. 'Yes,' he said quietly.

The door to de Tréville's room opened, and a man called out, 'Monsieur de Tréville will see Monsieur d'Artagnan.'

D'Artagnan went into the room. He was happy when the great man gave him his hand.

'I will talk to you in a minute,' said de Tréville. 'I have to do something now.' And he called out, 'Athos! Porthos! Aramis!'

Two musketeers came in.

'Where is Athos?' asked de Tréville.

'Athos is ill, sir, very ill,' said Aramis.

'Ill? What is wrong with him? Did somebody hurt him? Was there really a fight between six of the King's musketeers and six of the Cardinal's guards? You lost? That is bad – very bad! What is wrong with the musketeers?'

Porthos was angry. 'We did not see them. Before we could take out our swords, two of our men were dead. They hurt Athos badly. You know Athos well. He tried to get up, but he fell back. We fought, but they were six to three. Aramis broke his sword, but he took a sword from one of the Cardinal's men. He began to fight again. We did not run away.'

Then a man came to the door. He was a fine man, but he looked very ill. His face was white.

'Athos!' cried de Tréville and the two musketeers.

'You sent for me, sir,' said Athos – and fell to the floor.

'A doctor! Call a doctor!' said de Tréville. 'The King's doctor. The best doctor in Paris. Now!'

Porthos and Aramis ran out of the room and came back with a doctor. They took Athos away.

D'Artagnan was face to face with de Tréville.

'I am sorry about that,' said the great man. 'What can I do for you?'

'Sir,' said d'Artagnan, 'I had a letter . . .'

'It is all right. I know about you. Tell me – what can I do?'

'Sir, I came here because I wanted to be one of your musketeers. But I know now that only the best men can be musketeers.'

'Yes,' said de Tréville. 'First a man has to do well in one of the other companies.'

D'Artagnan was near a window. Suddenly he cried, 'There he is! He will not get away this time!' And he ran out of the room.

Chapter 3   Three Fights in a Day!

D'Artagnan ran from the room because he saw the man from
Meung through the window. He ran to the stairs, and into
another man in front of him. His head hit the other man's arm.

'I am sorry!' said d'Artagnan. 'I have to be quick.' He turned
to the stairs again.

A strong hand on his arm stopped him. It was Athos.

'You have to be quick?' said the musketeer. 'So you run into
me. Then you think that "sorry" makes everything all right? It
does not. We do things differently here. Are you from the country?'

D'Artagnan wanted to go downstairs, but he wasn't happy.

'Listen, sir,' he said. 'I *am* from the country, but you cannot
speak to me in that way!'

'Oh, can't I?'

'No! You cannot!' cried d'Artagnan. 'I cannot stop now,
but. . .'

'Perhaps you cannot stop now, sir, but you can find me
later.'

'Where can I find you?'

'Behind the church.'

'At what time?'

'About midday.'

'Midday? Right! I will be there.'

'And do not be late. I want to have your ears before a quarter
past twelve.'

'Right!' said d'Artagnan. And he started to run again. He
really wanted to catch the man from Meung.

Porthos was by the street door, but d'Artagnan didn't see him.
He pushed against him.

'I am sorry,' said d'Artagnan, 'but I have to catch somebody.'

'Perhaps you do have to catch somebody,' said the big man.
'But do not push musketeers, or somebody will hurt you.'

7

'Hurt me!' cried d'Artagnan. 'No man is going to hurt me!'

'At one o'clock, then, behind the Luxembourg.'

'At one o'clock! Right!' shouted d'Artagnan.

D'Artagnan ran outside as fast as he could. He looked for the man from Meung, but he couldn't see him anywhere.

'I will find him,' d'Artagnan thought, and he began to walk home. 'I have to fight two men. I will have to be careful now. I cannot fight any more men!'

A minute or two later, d'Artagnan saw Aramis with three of the King's guards. D'Artagnan went closer. A handkerchief fell, and Aramis put his foot on it.

'Your handkerchief, sir,' said d'Artagnan, and he tried to give it to Aramis. It was a very beautiful woman's handkerchief.

'Ho, ho!' cried a guard. 'She likes you, so she is giving you one of her handkerchiefs, Aramis!'

Aramis looked angry and began to walk away.

'Your handkerchief,' said d'Artagnan. He tried again to give it to the musketeer.

'Young Gascon,' said Aramis angrily, 'it is not my handkerchief.'

'I saw it fall.'

'So, you think I am wrong?'

'Yes, I do.' And d'Artagnan's hand went to his sword.

'Not here,' Aramis said. 'We cannot fight here. The Cardinal's guards are everywhere round here. Meet me at two o'clock at Monsieur de Tréville's house. I will take you to a nice quiet place from there.'

'Right!' said d'Artagnan.

He began to walk to the church. 'Now I am going to have three fights,' he thought. 'But when somebody kills me, he will be a musketeer.'

Chapter 4   The Cardinal's Guards

When d'Artagnan arrived at the church, Athos was there before him. Athos wasn't well.

He said, 'My friends are not here, but they will be here in a minute or two. Then we can start.'

'I have no friends here, sir,' d'Artagnan answered. 'I do not know anybody in Paris. I only know Monsieur de Tréville because my father gave me a letter for him.'

'Oh!' said Athos. 'That is bad. And you are very young. People will be angry with me when I kill you. They will think the fight was wrong. You have to have a friend here.'

'It is not really wrong,' said d'Artagnon. 'You are not strong because you are ill. Listen, I can give you something and you will get better quickly. My mother told me about it and it worked for me. It really is wonderful. You will be better in three days. Let's wait three days and have our fight then.'

D'Artagnan really wanted to help him, and Athos knew that. It was not because he didn't want to fight.

'That is kind of you,' said Athos. 'I will not take your help, but you are a good man. Where are my friends? Why are they not here?'

'Perhaps you have not got much time,' said d'Artagnan. 'Perhaps you would like to kill me as quickly as possible. We can start without them.'

'I like you,' answered Athos. 'Perhaps you will not die. Then I hope that we can be friends. Ah, here is one of my friends now!'

'What!' cried d'Artagnan. 'Is Monsieur Porthos one of your friends?'

'Yes. And there is my other friend.'

'What! Is Monsieur Aramis your other friend?'

'Yes, he is. There are always three of us. Everybody calls us the three musketeers.'

Athos looked at d'Artagnan and said to his friends, 'I am going to fight this man.'

'But I am going to fight him too,' cried Porthos.

'Yes,' said d'Artagnan. 'But at one o'clock.'

'And me?' asked Aramis.

'At two o'clock,' said d'Artagnan.

'Well, we can start now,' said Athos. 'When you are ready.'

D'Artagnan and Athos took out their swords. But suddenly five of the Cardinal's guards arrived with Monsieur de Jussac.

'The Cardinal's guards!' cried Porthos and Aramis. 'Put your swords away quickly.'

But it was too late.

'Stop fighting, musketeers,' said de Jussac. 'You know that you cannot fight. Give us your swords and come with us.'

'Sir,' said Aramis, 'only Monsieur de Tréville can stop us. Please go away.'

'You will come with us,' said de Jussac angrily.

Athos spoke very quietly. Only his friends and d'Artagnan could hear him.

'There are five of them and only three of us. We will lose again, and then we cannot go back to the Captain. We will have to die here.'

'Excuse me!' said d'Artagnan. 'Monsieur Athos says that there are only three of us. I think that we are four.'

The three musketeers looked at him. He was very young, but he was also quite strong.

'All right. And thank you,' said Athos. 'What is your name, young man?'

'D'Artagnan.'

'Right. We are Athos, Porthos, Aramis, and d'Artagnan now!'

The fight started. Athos fought Cahusac, one of the Cardinal's best swordsmen. Porthos fought Bicarat, and Aramis fought two of the guards. D'Artagnan was face to face with de Jussac.

The fight started.

De Jussac usually won his fights. He hoped to kill the young man quickly. Then he could help his friends. But the young man moved very quickly. De Jussac was angry. How could a young nobody fight the great de Jussac? Because he was angry, de Jussac began to do stupid things. He pushed his sword at the younger man. In that way he usually killed his man. But d'Artagnan turned de Jussac's sword away with his sword. It came under de Jussac's arm and went through him. De Jussac fell to the ground.

Aramis killed one of his two men, and turned to fight the other guard. Porthos hurt Bicarat and Bicarat hurt Porthos. But they enjoyed the fight. Athos fought well, but he was ill. He looked at d'Artagnan, and the young man ran to him.

D'Artagnan began to fight Cahusac, and Cahusac's sword flew out of his hand.

Aramis killed his second man, and Porthos could kill Bicarat at any time.

De Jussac was on the ground, but now he sat up.

'Stop!' he called to Bicarat.

The fight was at an end. The three musketeers and d'Artagnan carried the swords of the five Cardinal's guards to de Tréville. They were very happy.

Chapter 5   The Queen's Diamonds

Monsieur de Tréville was also very happy with his three musketeers and their new friend, d'Artagnan. He told the King about the fight, and the King was excited too.

'Talk to Monsieur des Essarts. He will have to find a place in his guards for this young Gascon,' said the King.

And so d'Artagnan was now one of the King's guards.

'Do well,' said de Tréville, 'and you can be one of the King's musketeers in a year or two.'

D'Artagnan was happy because now he had three friends in the musketeers – Athos, Porthos and Aramis.

The four men had many exciting times, many fights, and many laughs. Each man was always ready to help the others: 'One for all, all for one!'

◆

D'Artagnan was often a guard in the Queen's rooms. One of the Queen's women, Constance Bonacieux, was young and very pretty. D'Artagnan fell in love with her when he first saw her. She fell in love with him too. She told him about the Queen.

'The Queen is not happy,' she said. 'The King thinks that she is in love with the Duke of Buckingham. He is a very important man in England. The Cardinal hates the Queen and he wants the King to hate her too.'

The Queen liked the Duke of Buckingham very much, and she gave him some very fine diamond pins. She had them because the King gave them to her.

The Cardinal learned about the diamonds. He had people everywhere. They listened and told him everything. The Cardinal sent a woman, Milady, to England. She had to take some or all of the diamond pins from the Duke of Buckingham.

A letter came to the Cardinal from England.

I have got them. But I cannot leave London without more money. Send me some money, and I will be in Paris in five days.

The Cardinal spoke to the King. 'There is going to be a great dinner and dance here in Paris in twelve days' time. We would like you and the Queen to be there.'

'Oh, good!' said the King. He loved dances.

Then the Cardinal said: 'Please ask the Queen to wear her wonderful diamond pins.'

The next day, the King spoke to the Queen about the dance and about the diamonds.

'Did the Cardinal plan the dinner and the dance?' the Queen asked.

'Yes.'

'And I have to wear the diamonds? That was the Cardinal's idea too?'

'Yes – yes, it was.'

When the King went back to his rooms, the Queen started to cry. 'What can I do?' she thought. 'The Cardinal knows everything. The King does not know now, but he will. The Cardinal will tell him. I cannot send anybody to Buckingham. The Cardinal will stop them.'

'I think I can help,' said Constance Bonacieux. 'Are you unhappy about the diamond pins? Is that the problem? The Duke of Buckingham has them and we have to get them back?'

The Queen looked at the pretty face. Constance's eyes were kind, and the Queen thought, 'Constance wants to help me. She does not work for the Cardinal.'

'Yes,' the Queen said, 'but how can we get them back?'

'We will have to send somebody to the Duke.'

'Who? Who will go? And I will have to send a letter. But I cannot do that. The Cardinal will find it and that will be the end of me. The King will send me away.'

Constance said, 'I know somebody. He will take the letter to England, and he will not tell the Cardinal.'

Chapter 6   To England for the Queen

Constance Bonacieux, of course, gave the Queen's letter to d'Artagnan.

D'Artagnan was very happy. 'Constance loves me!' he thought. 'I will leave now,' he cried.

'The King will send me away.'

'Here is some money for your journey,' she said, and she gave him a bag of money.

D'Artagnan went to de Tréville and said, 'I have to do something for the Queen. It is important for her good name, and perhaps for her life.'

De Tréville said, 'What do you want from me? Tell me. I will help.'

'Please ask Monsieur des Essarts to give me fourteen days. I will have to go away for that time.'

'Where are you going? Can you tell me?'

'To London.'

'Who wants to stop you?'

'The Cardinal, I think.'

'I will send your three friends with you. We will say that Athos is ill. Porthos and Aramis have to help him, so they are going too. I will give you some permits. The permits will say that they have to go to the sea. It will be good for Athos there.'

'Thank you, sir.'

When their permits came from de Tréville, the three musketeers wanted to know everything.

'What is this journey for?' asked Porthos.

'We are going to London,' d'Artagnan told them. 'But I cannot tell you much. I have to take a letter to London. It is here in my bag. The Cardinal will try to stop me, and perhaps his men will kill me. Then one of you will have to take the letter. One of us has to get to London with the letter.'

◆

At two o'clock in the morning the four friends left Paris. They arrived at Chantilly at eight o'clock in the morning, and had breakfast at an inn. But when they were ready to leave, a man spoke to Porthos. 'Drink to the Cardinal,' he said.

Porthos did this, and then he asked the other man to drink to the King. The man took out his sword, and cried, 'I know no king, only the Cardinal!'

'I know that you have to fight this man,' Athos said to Porthos. 'That is all right. We will wait for you for two hours at Beauvais.'

They waited at Beauvais, but Porthos did not come.

'There are only three of us now,' said Athos.

After only a short time on the road they had to go past some trees. Suddenly, eight men with muskets attacked them from the trees. One of them hit Aramis and hurt him badly.

'We cannot stop and fight them,' cried d'Artagnan. 'There is no time.'

But at Crèvecoeur, Athos and d'Artagnan had to leave Aramis at an inn.

The two men arrived at Amiens at midnight and stopped at another inn. In the morning d'Artagnan found the horses and Athos paid the innkeeper. Then d'Artagnan saw four or five men with swords and guns. The men ran into the inn. There was a noise, and then Athos shouted, 'They have got me! Get away, quickly!'

D'Artagnan had to leave him there.

When he was nearly in Calais, his horse fell. After that, he had to walk.

D'Artagnan arrived in Calais and found the ships. He listened to the captain of one of the ships. The captain was with another man.

'I would like to take you across to England,' the captain said. 'But from this morning, nobody can go on a ship without a permit from the Cardinal.'

'I have got a permit,' the man said. 'Here it is.'

'All right, Monsieur le Comte★. Take it to the office. The man there will put his name on it and then we can go. The office is in that street there.'

★ Comte: the French word for a count, an important man in France at that time.

The man started to walk quickly. D'Artagnan ran after him and stopped him in the quiet street.

'Are you going somewhere?' he asked.

'Yes, I am. Get out of my way.'

'Of course. But I want your permit from the Cardinal.'

The man took out his sword and tried to kill d'Artagnan. But d'Artagnan was too quick for him. He took out his sword and with it he turned the other man's sword away. D'Artagnan's sword went through the man, and he fell to the ground.

D'Artagnan found the Cardinal's permit. It was for the 'Comte de Wardes'. He took it to the office. The man there didn't know the Comte de Wardes, so he put his name on the permit. Then d'Artagnan went back to the ship.

He paid the captain some money, and in a short time he was at sea, on his way to England.

D'Artagnan knew no English, but he found somebody at Dover. This man could speak French, and he helped d'Artagnan to get a horse. After that, he showed him the right road for London.

When d'Artagnan arrived there, he wrote the Duke of Buckingham's name on a piece of paper. Then he showed it to people. Everybody knew the great man's house.

Chapter 7   The Duke of Buckingham

'A letter for the Duke?' said a man at the door.'Give it to me.'

'No,' said d'Artagnan.'I have to give it to the Duke.'

'A letter for the Duke?" said a man inside the house. 'I will take it to him.'

'No,' said d'Artagnan.

In the end he saw the Duke.

'What do you have to tell me?' asked the Duke.'Is something wrong? Is it the Queen?'

And from the Duke's words, d'Artagnan knew. He loved the Queen. D'Artagnan put his hand inside his coat and pulled out the Queen's letter.

'Read this,' he said.

The Duke read the letter and then went quickly to a box. He took out the wonderful diamond pins.

'These are the Queen's diamonds,' he said. 'She gave them to me, but now she wants them again. She has to have them as quickly as possible.'

He looked again at the diamonds and suddenly he shouted, 'Oh no! There were twelve pins, but now there are only ten! Two are not here.'

'Not here?' said d'Artagnan.

'Yes, look. But who did it? Let me think. Ah, yes, I remember now. I wore the diamonds at a dinner and Lady de Winter was there. She spoke to me two or three times, and that was strange. She works for the Cardinal, and she does not like me. So she has two of the diamond pins. That is bad, but we can do something about it. I will have to buy two more diamond pins, and they will have to look the same.'

So the Duke paid a man, and the man made two more diamond pins.

◆

Two days later, d'Artagnan started on his journey back to Paris.

The Duke of Buckingham's men worked hard. A ship took d'Artagnan to the small French town of St Valéry. He found a very fine horse there, and there were three other horses at inns on the road to Paris. The journey from St Valéry to Paris was about twelve hours.

When he arrived in Paris, d'Artagnan went to de Tréville's house. De Tréville asked no questions.

'You can sleep here tonight,' he said.

Chapter 8   The Great Dinner

The next day, everybody in Paris was excited about the dinner and dance. When the King arrived, the great and rich men and women of Paris were there. The King didn't look happy.

The Queen arrived five minutes later. She, too, looked sad – or was she only tired?

The Cardinal met her. There were no diamonds on her! Suddenly he looked really happy. He spoke to the King.

'Ask the Queen about her diamonds. You remember – you wanted her to wear them.'

The King looked very angry. He went to the Queen and said: 'Why aren't you wearing your diamonds?'

'I did not want to lose them on the way here, but I will put them on now.'

'Please do that.' The King left her, and the Queen went to another room.

The Cardinal gave the King a box. There were two diamond pins in it.

'What does this mean?' the King asked.

'The Queen says that she has her diamonds. I do not think that she has. Look at her when she comes back. How many pins is she wearing? Only ten, I think. Ask her about the other two.'

The King looked at the Cardinal. He wanted to ask more questions. But suddenly the Queen was there again. She had a different dress now, and she looked very beautiful. On her dress there were twelve diamond pins.

The Cardinal's face went dark red, and he looked angry and afraid. The Queen had the diamonds – but were there twelve or only ten?

The King walked across to his wife.

'Thank you,' he said. 'You put the diamonds on very quickly. But did you not lose two pins? Here they are.' He gave the Queen the Cardinal's two pins.

The Cardinal looked angry and afraid.

'I do not understand,' said the Queen. 'Are you giving me two more diamond pins? Then I will have fourteen!'

The King looked at the pins on her dress. Twelve! He turned and called the Cardinal to him. He was very, very angry. Everybody knew that, but nobody could hear his words to the Cardinal.

Was that a smile on the Queen's face?

◆

Later that night, d'Artagnan was on guard at the Queen's rooms.

'Please come with me. Be very quiet.' It was Constance Bonacieux. She took him into a small dark room next to a much bigger room. He could hear somebody in the bigger room.

Constance left him. After a minute, the door opened a little, and d'Artagnan saw an arm – a very beautiful arm.

He took the lovely white hand. It was the Queen's hand, and she pushed something into his hand. Then the arm went back through the door.

After a time Constance came and took him back into the light. D'Artagnan opened his hand. In it was a beautiful diamond.

Chapter 9   D'Artagnan's Friends

D'Artagnan left Paris again, because he wanted to find his friends. At Chantilly, the innkeeper was happy to see him.

'Yes,' he said, 'your friend is here. He is nearly better. Well – he lost the fight. But he does not want anybody to know that.'

'Lost the fight? What fight? You will have to tell me now.'

'The fight finished very quickly. The other man's sword went into Monsieur Porthos before he could do anything. Then the man asked Monsieur Porthos his name. When he heard it, he said: "What! Not d'Artagnan?" He helped Monsieur Porthos to his feet and then he left my inn.'

D'Artagnan went up and found his friend. The big man was in bed, but he had a plate of food and a bottle of wine.

'Oh, there you are!' he said. 'Do you know about the fight?'

'No. What happened? The innkeeper told me your room number, and here I am. We waited for you at Beauvais but you did not come.'

'Oh, I taught a man to use a sword, but I caught my foot on something. When I fell, I hurt my leg badly.'

'And the other man?'

'Oh, he left.'

D'Artagnan asked, 'Will you be all right here? I have to go and look for the other musketeers.'

'You go and find them,' said Porthos. 'I will be fine.' He looked happily at his food and his bottle.

◆

At Crèvecoeur, d'Artagnan went to the inn. The innkeeper there was a woman.

'Can you tell me about my friend?' he asked her. 'I left him here last week.'

'A fine young man of about twenty-five? He is here now. A really nice man!'

'Good. I will go and see him.'

'I do not think you can see him now, sir. Two important men from the church are with him.'

'Why?' cried d'Artagnan. 'Is he very ill? Is he dying?'

'No, sir. He is better. But he wants to be a man of the Church.'

D'Artagnan ran to Aramis's room. Aramis looked round when the door opened.

'Ah!' he said, but he was not really excited. 'D'Artagnan!'

'Are you coming back to Paris with me?' asked d'Artagnan.

'Well, no. I am going to go into the Church. My two friends here are going to help me.'

'Oh!' said d'Artagnan. He thought for a minute. 'So you will not want the letter?'

'What letter?'

'It came for you when you were away. It is from Tours, and it has the same name on it as that handkerchief.'

'Where is it?' cried Aramis.

'I have it here somewhere . . .' he laughed.

Aramis cried, 'Find it! Find it!'

D'Artagnan found the letter quite easily. Aramis opened it quickly and read it.

'Oh, d'Artagnan! She loves me! Oh, I am very happy!' He took d'Artagnan by the hand, and they danced round the two men from the Church.

'Now we have to find Athos,' said d'Artagnan. But when Aramis climbed on his horse, he cried out.

'You start back slowly to Paris,' said d'Artagnan, 'and I will find Athos.'

D'Artagnan liked Athos the best of the three musketeers. Athos was quiet and intelligent, but he enjoyed laughing with his friends.

At Amiens, d'Artagnan pushed his way into the noisy inn. 'Where is my friend? I left him here,' he shouted at the innkeeper.

'I did not do anything. The men – about eight of them – attacked him. He killed two of them with his musket, and another with his sword . . .'

'Where is he?'

'He is in the wine cupboard, sir. He went in and shut the door. Then he put heavy boxes behind it.'

'What!' shouted d'Artagnan. 'Is he in there now?'

'Yes, sir, yes! He will not come out. We want to get in there for more wine.'

'Where is the door?' The man took him to it. 'Athos!' called d'Artagnan. 'You can come out now. There is only me here.'

D'Artagnan could hear noises in the cupboard – Athos moved the heavy boxes. Then the door opened and Athos came out. He had a bottle under each arm.

The innkeeper brought food to them and then went to the cupboard. 'My wine! My food! Where is it?' he cried.

D'Artagnan told Athos about Porthos and Aramis.

'I found Porthos in bed with a bad leg,' he said. 'And then I found Aramis with two men from the Church.'

'And what happened to you?' asked Athos.

'I am in love with Constance.'

'That is bad,' said Athos.

'But you always say that. You know nothing about love.'

So then Athos told d'Artagnan about his 'friend'. This 'friend' met a very beautiful girl. She was beautiful and very intelligent. He married her, and for months he was very happy. But then he began to learn things about her. She was not very kind to people, and Athos's 'friend' did not like this. Then he learned more. She was a bad woman in every way.

'So I will never fall in love again. That woman is Lady de Winter – they call her "Milady".'

D'Artagnan understood. The 'friend' in Athos's story was not really a friend at all. The story was about Athos, and Milady was his wife!

Chapter 10   Milady's Plans

The Huguenots* had the city of La Rochelle. King Louis XIII and Cardinal Richelieu wanted to take it back, so they sent an army there. The Cardinal went first with the army, and the King followed with his musketeers and guards.

* Huguenots: French Protestants. Most French people were Catholics.

On their way to La Rochelle, Athos, Porthos and Aramis stopped at an inn near the city. They heard a lot of noise at the top of the stairs, and the innkeeper asked for their help.

'There is a woman up there,' he said, 'and three men are trying to get into her room.'

The three musketeers quickly sent the three men away. Then they had a drink and left. Suddenly they saw two men on horses. The men came nearer and then stopped.

Athos called: 'Who is there?'

One of the men called back: 'Who are you?'

'That is not an answer,' called Athos. 'I said "Who is there?" Answer now or you will be sorry.'

'I will not be sorry. Why are you here at this time of night?'

He was an important man. Athos could hear that.

'We are King's Musketeers,' he said.

'Your name?' said the other man. He had his hand over his face.

'Show us your face,' said Athos.

The man took his hand away and showed his face. It was the Cardinal.

'Your name?' the Cardinal said again.

'Athos.'

'So the two men with you are Porthos and Aramis?'

'Yes, sir.'

'Then please follow me. But what are you doing here?'

Athos told him about the fight at the inn. 'The three men wanted to push their way into the woman's room,' he said.

'This woman,' said the Cardinal, 'was she young and pretty?'

'We did not see her, sir,' Athos answered.

'Oh, good. Well, I am on my way to the inn now. Come with me.'

At the inn the Cardinal spoke to the innkeeper. 'Show these men to a room,' he said. 'They can wait there.'

Porthos and Aramis started to play a game of cards, but Athos couldn't sit quietly. He walked round the room. Then he stopped and stood near the fireplace. He could hear people in the room above. He heard the Cardinal: 'This is very important, Milady. We have to do it right.'

'Milady!' Athos said very quietly. Porthos and Aramis stopped playing and went to him.

'What can I do for you now, sir?' said a woman.

When he heard her, Athos's face went white.

The Cardinal said, 'A ship is waiting for you at the mouth of the Charente river. Go to London again. When you get there, visit the Duke of Buckingham.'

Milady said, 'But he will know about the diamond pins. He will not listen to me.'

'This time you are going to speak to him openly for me and for France. I know that he is planning to send ships and men to the Protestants at La Rochelle. I do not want him to send them. Say that I know about his love for the Queen. I know that he meets her. Say that I will tell the King and everybody.'

'Perhaps that will not stop him,' Milady answered.

'Then you know that he has to die.'

Milady said nothing for a minute, then: 'All right, sir. I understand. I will do that for you. Now will you do something for me? I want some people to die too.'

'Who?'

'Constance Bonacieux and d'Artagnan.'

The Cardinal did not understand. 'Why d'Artagnan? He is a fine man.'

'Yes, but dangerous. He fought your guards with the King's musketeers and won. He killed my lover, the Comte de Wardes. He helped the Queen with the diamond pins . . .'

'All right. Give me a pen and paper,' said the Cardinal.

◆

When the Cardinal came down again, Athos said to him, 'When we leave here, please let me go before you, sir. Porthos and Aramis will go with you. Then we can guard you well.'

'Yes,' said the Cardinal. 'Do that.'

So Athos left quickly, but a little way down the road he turned into the trees. He waited, and the Cardinal and the men with him went past. Then he went quickly back to the inn.

Milady was afraid when she saw the musketeer. Then he came nearer, and her face went white.

'You know me, then,' said Athos.

'You are not dead!'

'No. I am not dead – but your second husband is. Then de Winter married you, and he is dead too. You killed them for their money.'

'What do you want?'

'The Cardinal wrote a permit for you. Give it to me.'

She saw the gun in his hand, and she gave him the piece of paper. Athos opened it and read :

The person with this letter in his hand
is helping me and France.
3 December 1627   Richelieu

Chapter 11   Breakfast at the Bastion

'We have to talk.'

D'Artagnan looked at Athos's face. It was important.

'We can go to the Parpaillot inn for breakfast,' he said. 'The walls there will be thicker than here.'

So the four friends went to the inn. But there were a lot of other people there. King's guards, the Cardinal's guards, musketeers, Swiss guards and other men came in and out.

Athos said, 'This is not a good place. We will have to wait. D'Artagnan, tell us about your night and we will tell you about ours later.'

De Busigny, a guard from their company, was near them. He heard Athos's last words and said, 'Yes, did you have a fight at La Rochelle last night?'

'Did you not attack a bastion?' asked a Swiss guard.

'Yes, we took the St Gervais bastion,' answered d'Artagnan, 'and we killed some guards there.'

Suddenly Athos said, 'Do you want to put your money on something?'

'On what?' asked de Busigny.

'I say that I and my three friends are going to have breakfast in the St Gervais bastion. We will stay there for one hour.'

'And I say that you cannot do it,' said de Busigny. 'They will attack you. How much money are you putting on it?'

'There are four of us and four of you. Perhaps a very good dinner for eight people? The losers will pay for the dinner. What do you say?'

'Very good,' said de Busigny and the other men.

'Your breakfast is ready,' the innkeeper called.

'We will take it with us,' said Athos.

When they left the inn, d'Artagnan asked, 'What is this about?'

Athos said, 'We have to make some important plans. We could not talk at the inn.'

◆

They arrived at the bastion, and the four friends looked back at the French army. Two or three hundred men were there. De Busigny and his three friends were with them.

Athos took his hat, put it on the end of his sword, and pushed it high above his head. The French army shouted happily when they saw that.

There were twelve or more dead men in the bastion.

'Now,' said Athos, 'let's get the guns and musket balls from these dead men. We can talk at the same time. These dead men are not listening to us. How many muskets are there?'

'Twelve,' said Aramis. 'And about a hundred musket balls.'

'Good,' said Athos. 'Let's get the guns. Then we will eat.'

'But what do you want to tell us?' d'Artagnan asked.

'Well, I saw Milady last night.'

'What! You saw your ...'

Athos put up his hand. 'Be careful. The others do not know as much as you do. Milady has a permit from the Cardinal. She wants to kill you, d'Artagnan.'

Chapter 12   Attack!

Aramis looked out at La Rochelle. 'About twenty men are coming, but some of them are workmen,' he said. 'They are going to build the walls again.'

'Where are they?' asked Athos.

'About 500 metres away.'

'Good. We can finish this bottle of wine.'

When there was no more wine in the bottle, Athos stood up.

'Let's send them away,' he said. Then he called, 'My good men, some friends and I are having breakfast in this bastion. Please go away and come back later.'

'They are going to attack!' cried d'Artagnan.

'I know.' said Athos. 'But they are not very good, so they will not hit us.'

Four musket balls hit the bastion all round Athos, but they did not hit him. The four friends took up their muskets. Three of the attackers fell dead, and the musketeers hurt another man. The workmen ran back to the town.

'Please go away and come back later.'

'Let's finish our breakfast,' said Athos, 'but one of us will have to watch for an attack. We will now tell d'Artagnan about last night.'

Next, about twenty-five men came from La Rochelle to the bastion.

'There are a lot of them,' said Porthos. 'Can we stop them?'

'We have to,' said Athos. 'We have to finish breakfast. Ten more minutes. We said an hour — remember? We will use all the muskets. Then we will push this wall down on top of them.'

The musketeers fought well, and ten men from La Rochelle died. The other men started to climb up the bastion, but the four friends pushed the wall down. It was weak from the attack the night before. The men below shouted loudly.

'Have we really killed all of them?' Aramis asked.

'No,' said Porthos. 'Four or five are going back to La Rochelle.'

'They will send half their army next time,' said d'Artagnan.

'Well, we will have to use *our* army,' said Athos. 'We can use these men.' And he pushed a dead man on to the inside wall of the bastion and put a musket by him. The other three laughed and did the same with the other dead men.

Then Athos said, 'Milady is Lady de Winter. She killed her husband, and he was a friend of the Duke of Buckingham. Milady is on her way to England now. We have to tell the Duke about this. Can we get a letter to him?'

'Yes,' said d'Artagnan. 'There is a man at St Valéry. He can take it to him.'

They were very happy with their little army of dead men.

'The men from La Rochelle will go more slowly when they see our army,' said Athos. 'And here they come!'

Large numbers of men from La Rochelle began to move nearer to the bastion. They came slowly and carefully.

'It's an hour now,' said Athos. 'We can go. Let's tell our friends first.'

The four friends stood high on the walls of the bastion. The men from La Rochelle tried to hit them, but they couldn't. The musket balls didn't come near them.

The French army watched. There were 2,000 men or more there now.

Athos, Porthos, Aramis and d'Artagnan walked back to their army. They laughed when they heard a sudden great noise from behind them.

'They are trying to kill the dead men,' said Aramis.

'Yes,' said Athos. 'And the dead men will not attack. So they will think it is a clever plan, and they will talk about it first. We have a lot of time.'

The three friends walked back slowly. The French army watched them and shouted loudly.

The Cardinal sent Houdinière, the captain of his guards. He asked the musketeers about the noise.

'What is happening?' the Cardinal asked, when Houdinière came back.

'Three musketeers and a guard had breakfast at the St Gervais bastion. And when they were there, they killed a lot of men from La Rochelle, sir.'

The Cardinal asked, 'What are the names of the musketeers?'

'Athos, Porthos and Aramis, sir.'

'Those three again! And the guard?'

'Monsieur d'Artagnan.'

'Him again!'

Chapter 13   The New Lieutenant

When Milady's ship arrived at Portsmouth, a young man climbed on to it from an English boat. He spoke to the captain and then said to Milady, 'Please come with me.'

He and his men took her to a room in a big house, and then they left. After a time, another man came in.

Milady looked at him. 'De Winter!' she cried. 'Oh, no!'

'Yes,' answered de Winter, 'your second husband's brother. You married him and then killed him. And your first husband was not dead. Now you have to die for that.'

◆

Houdinière, the captain of the Cardinal's guards, found Athos, Porthos, Aramis and d'Artagnan in an inn.

'Monsieur d'Artagnan, please come with me to the Cardinal now,' he said.

That night, when the Cardinal came back to his house, he found d'Artagnan and his three friends at his door.

D'Artagnan was without his sword, but the other three had swords and guns.

'Come with me, Monsieur d'Artagnan,' the Cardinal said.

'We will wait for you, d'Artagnan,' said Athos.

The Cardinal heard him and stopped for a minute. Then he went into the house and into his office without a word. D'Artagnan followed him.

They were the only two people in the room, and there was a table between them. The Cardinal said, 'Why are you here? Do you know?'

'No, sir. What did I do?'

'Better men than you lost their heads for these things,' said the Cardinal angrily.

'What things?' asked d'Artagnan quietly.

'You spoke to the Duke of Buckingham, and sent him a letter. You took and used a permit from me...'

'Yes, sir. A very bad woman told you these things. This woman married and killed two men. And her first husband was not dead.'

'What are you saying?' the Cardinal cried. 'Which woman are you talking about?'

'Lady de Winter – Milady!'

'I did not know about her husbands. Where is she now?'

'Dead, sir.'

'What!'

'She is dead.'

'Dead? You are saying that she is dead? Who killed her?'

'In a way, my friends and I did.'

The Cardinal looked at the young man, but d'Artagnan was not afraid.

'Then you will have to die,' he said. 'You were wrong to kill her.'

'But I have a piece of paper. It says that everything is all right,' d'Artagnan said.

'A piece of paper?'

'Yes, sir.'

'And who put his name on it? The King?'

'No,' answered d'Artagnan. 'It has your name on it.'

He pulled out the piece of paper and gave it to the Cardinal. It was Milady's permit from the Cardinal.

Richelieu read it:

The person with this letter in his hand
is helping me and France.
3 December 1627   Richelieu

He read it again carefully. He sat and thought for a minute or two. Then he threw away the piece of paper.

'Well,' d'Artagnan thought, 'I am not afraid to die.'

The Cardinal stood up slowly and walked to the table.

He wrote something on a piece of paper and put his name on it. Then he gave it to d'Artagnan.

35

'Take this paper. Look at it. There is no name on it, so you can write in the name.'

D'Artagnan looked at it quickly.

It was a paper for a new lieutenant in the musketeers! But there was no name on it.

The Cardinal said, 'You are a good man, d'Artagnan. Write your name on it. But remember – I gave it to you.' Then he called, 'Rochefort!'

The important man from Meung came in.

'Rochefort,' said the Cardinal. 'You see Monsieur d'Artagnan here. Well, now he is my friend. So, stop fighting. Give him your hand.'

That evening d'Artagnan visited Athos. He wanted to give the paper to him.

'No,' said Athos. 'The Cardinal wants you to be a lieutenant. You will be a good one.'

Next d'Artagnan visited Porthos. 'I want to give you something,' he said.

'What is that?' Porthos asked.

'This paper,' d'Artagnan answered. 'Write your name on it.'

Porthos looked at it and then gave it back to d'Artagnan.

'No,' he said. 'It is yours. You take it.'

So the young man visited Aramis.

'Thank you, but no,' said Aramis. 'You have it. You will do well in the army.'

D'Artagnan went back to Athos's rooms.

'The other two will not take the paper,' he said.

'Because it is for you,' Athos said. He took his pen, and on the paper he wrote the name 'd'Artagnan'.

ACTIVITIES

Chapters 1–4

Before you read

1 Read the Introduction.
   a Which city does d'Artagnan want to go to?
   b Why does he want to go there?
   c What is a *musketeer*? What does he carry?
2 Find these words in your dictionary. They are all in the story.
   army attack captain cardinal carriage duke guard
   hankerchief inn innkeeper king piece sword
   a Which are words for a person or people?
   b Finish these sentences with other words.
      – Now we go by car; in the past people used a ..... .
      – You could eat and sleep at an ..... .
      – People often fought with a ..... .
   c Answer these questions.
      – What do you do if a dog *attacks* you?
      – Where is your *handkerchief* now?
      – Do you write new English words in a notebook or on a *piece*
        of paper?

After you read

3 How do these people feel? Why?
   a D'Artagnan, about the man from Meung?
   b De Tréville, about his musketeers?
   c The three musketeers, about d'Artagnan?
4 You are de Jussac. Why did you lose the fight with the four
   friends? Tell the Cardinal.

Chapters 5–9

Before you read

5 The beautiful young woman at Meung is important to the story.
   Who do you think she is?

6 Find these words in your dictionary.

diamond   permit   pin   queen

Which:

a shines in the light?

b is the King's wife?

c can you wear on your dress?

d is a piece of paper?

After you read

7 Answer these questions.

a Why is the Queen unhappy when the King wants her to wear her diamonds?

b Why does Milady go to England?

c D'Artagnan can't speak English. How does he find the Duke of Buckingham?

d How many diamond pins are there at the Cardinal's dinner? Why?

8 Work with another student. Have the conversation between the Queen and Constance after the dinner and dance. What does the Queen want to do now?

Chapters 10–13

Before you read

9 How will the story end? Will d'Artagnan die before the end of the story? What will happen to Milady?

10 Look at these sentences. What are the words in *italics* in your language?

a A *bastion* is a place with strong, high walls. It is difficult to attack it.

b A *lieutenant* is a person in the army, below a captain.

After you read

11 Who is speaking? Who are they talking to? What are they talking about?

a 'A ship is waiting for you at the mouth of the Charente river.'

b 'You are not dead!'

    c 'Please go away and come back later.'

    d 'Now you have to die for that.'

    e 'Write your name on it.'

12 What do you think of Milady? What words can you use for her? Was it right for her to die? Why (not)?

Writing

13 You are d'Artagnan. Write a letter to your father on your first day in Paris. Tell him about your journey.

14 Which person in the story is the most interesting? Why? Write about them.

15 What do you think is going to happen to d'Artagnan? Write about his life a year after the end of the story.

16 Why do people enjoy the story 160 years after Dumas wrote it? What is good about it?

Answers for the Activities in this book are available from your local office or alternatively write to: Penguin Readers Marketing Department, Pearson Education, Edinburgh Gate, Harlow, Essex CM20 2JE.